DRAKE
and the
ARMADA

DRAKE
and the
ARMADA

Written by Fiona Macdonald
Illustrated by Chris Molan
Consultant, Crispin Gill

Hampstead Press New York 1988

Introduction

This book tells the story of Sir Francis Drake, a famous 16th-century sailor, explorer and battle commander. Drake was born into a poor family, but his skill as a sailor and his many exploits made him famous throughout Europe. In England, Drake became a national hero after helping to defeat the Spanish Armada in 1588.

Although this book reads like a story, it is based on evidence collected by historians about Drake's life and the quarrels between England and Spain during the 16th century. This evidence comes from government papers and reports, letters (Drake was a great letter-writer), old maps, drawings and books. Where possible, the words spoken and written by the characters in this book are taken from these old documents, although the language and spelling have been modernized. In places, however, it has been necessary to imagine what might have been said – for example, we know very little about Drake's childhood. We are not even sure when he was born! All the pictures are based on the evidence of real ships, guns and buildings of the 16th century, and on contemporary portraits of Drake, Hawkins, Queen Elizabeth of England and King Philip of Spain.

In his lifetime, everyone agreed that Drake was an extremely skillful sailor, and that he was a good master to his men. We also know, from his letters, that Drake believed that God was guiding him in his battles against the Spaniards. Of course, that did not stop him enjoying the wealth and popularity that his raids on Spanish shipping brought him! In the 16th century, most people believed that it was right to fight and kill people who did not share your religious beliefs, especially if they also interfered with your overseas trade or threatened your country.

You will find various dates in this book. You may find that they differ by 11 days from dates in other history books. This is because there are two ways of dating events before 1752. One way, called Old Style, gives the dates as they were thought of at the time of the event. The other, known as New Style, uses the corrected, "modern" way of giving dates. The system was changed from Old to New Styles because, by 1751, people realized that they had been measuring time incorrectly, and that the dates on their calendars were 11 days out of step with "real" time, as measured by the sun, moon and stars. Therefore, in 1752, the calendar was changed by the government, moving forward by 11 days. Dates in this book are New Style.

You will find a glossary at the end of the book. This will help you with unfamiliar words and will explain a little more about some of the places, people and ships mentioned in the book.

Contents

Growing up on board ship

The evening sunlight slanted across the calm waters of the harbor. Two sailors emerged from the smoky darkness of an inn, and sat down on the quayside. "So he's dead, then," said the older one, taking a sip of his beer. "I can't believe it! Sir Francis Drake, dead and gone. We'll never see his like again." He sighed. "I can remember, my lad, how proud we Devon men were when Drake came back from his round-the-world voyage. And how we celebrated when we defeated the great Spanish Armada!" The old man shook his head mournfully. "He was a fine sailor, and a great hero. He made me feel proud to be an Englishman! However long you live, you won't find another skipper like him!"

It was the summer of 1551, over 40 years before that conversation outside the inn. Young Francis Drake tossed and turned on his prickly straw mattress. It was a hot, sultry night and he was dreaming. Coming toward him, he saw rough men armed with knives and pitchforks. Their faces were grim. They were hunting, and they meant to kill. "We

must escape!" he muttered. "They're after us! Look! The town is on fire!" He kicked off his blankets. "They've got swords! Help! Father! Help!" He shouted so loudly that he woke himself up. He opened his eyes. It was pitch dark. Where was he?

In his dream, Francis had been back in Devon, reliving the terrifying day when his family had to leave their home after Catholic rebels attacked everyone who did not share their beliefs. Francis's father was a Protestant preacher, and so his family had been forced to flee for their lives. Perhaps now the rebels had caught up with them at last . . .

Cautiously, Francis sat up and rubbed his eyes. He took a deep breath. He was safe! He was hundreds of miles from Devon, and that evil time was long gone. He was sleeping next to his brothers below decks in the converted hulk that was their new home. It was moored on the River Medway, in sight of the great ships at anchor in the royal dockyards of Chatham. He heard his mother stirring in the next cabin. "Is that you, Francis?" she called. "Were you dreaming? Try to get back to sleep if you can. Remember, it's Sunday tomorrow. You've got to be up early to row your father across the river to his prayer meeting."

Dreams of the future

Young Francis and his brothers were raised to be as much at home on water as on dry land. They learned to understand the winds and tides, and how to handle a boat on the busy river. By the time he was 15, Francis had found work helping the captain of a small sailing vessel. Together they made voyages to France and the Low Countries, carrying loads of grain, cloth and leather.

Then, one day, the old captain fell sick. On his deathbed, he called Francis to him. "You must have my ship when I am gone," he said. "With her, you'll be able to earn your own living. Look after her, won't you? She's served me well."

Francis never forgot the old man's generosity. He took the ship, and carried on the trade his master had taught him. But somehow he felt dissatisfied. "Surely," he thought, "there's more to life than this? I'm not yet 20. Do I want to spend my life sailing back and forth across the English Channel?"

Then, one day while he was supervising the unloading of his cargo, he overheard a conversation that set his mind racing. "So you see," said a loud, confident voice, with a strong West country accent, "investing in my next voyage to the West Indies will bring you real profits! All London will want to buy the gold and pearls I'll bring back. And there'll be sugar and spices, too. You'll make your fortunes! All I need now are men with vision, like yourselves, to back me, and lend me the money I need to make my ship ready to sail. I promise you, I'll bring you back a whole shipload of treasure."

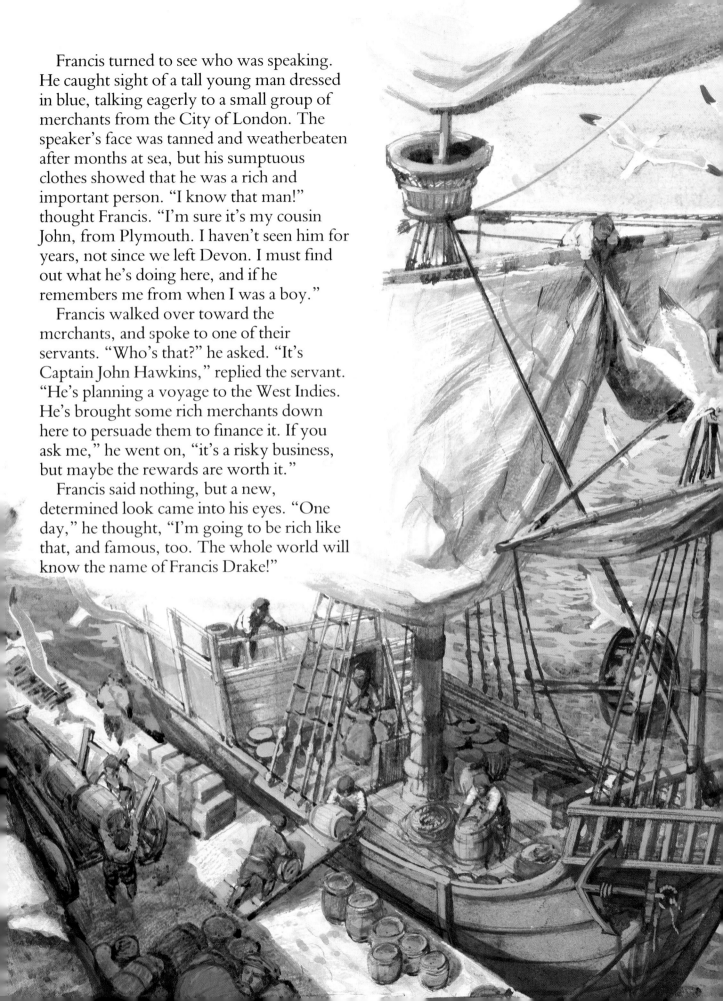

Francis turned to see who was speaking. He caught sight of a tall young man dressed in blue, talking eagerly to a small group of merchants from the City of London. The speaker's face was tanned and weatherbeaten after months at sea, but his sumptuous clothes showed that he was a rich and important person. "I know that man!" thought Francis. "I'm sure it's my cousin John, from Plymouth. I haven't seen him for years, not since we left Devon. I must find out what he's doing here, and if he remembers me from when I was a boy."

Francis walked over toward the merchants, and spoke to one of their servants. "Who's that?" he asked. "It's Captain John Hawkins," replied the servant. "He's planning a voyage to the West Indies. He's brought some rich merchants down here to persuade them to finance it. If you ask me," he went on, "it's a risky business, but maybe the rewards are worth it."

Francis said nothing, but a new, determined look came into his eyes. "One day," he thought, "I'm going to be rich like that, and famous, too. The whole world will know the name of Francis Drake!"

Spanish treachery

"This heat is unbearable!" Drake mopped his sweaty face on his shirtsleeve. All around, vicious mosquitos buzzed in the heavy air. It had been a long, dangerous voyage, first to Africa, to pick up slaves, and then to the West Indies, to sell them to the Spanish settlers there. Now, after a brief skirmish with the Spanish naval garrison, they were anchored off the island of San Juan de Ulua, hoping to repair their storm-damaged ships.

Suddenly, brisk footsteps sounded on the stairway. The men sprang to their feet. Captain John Hawkins, that proud figure Drake had so admired on the London quayside, strode across the deck. He was furious. "That fool of a Spanish governor won't let us shelter here any longer," he snapped. "Says it's against his orders!"

But there was much worse to come for Hawkins and his crew. A Spanish fleet sailed into San Juan, ready to unload supplies from Spain. "Our only chance is to make a deal with them," explained Hawkins. Drake listened carefully. He was learning a lot on this voyage as one of Hawkins's captains. "We'll try to buy time, and then make our

escape. Much as I'd like to attack them, we wouldn't stand a chance. Anyway," he added bitterly, "it might not please the queen. We don't want to be executed as pirates the moment we get home!"

Hawkins went to negotiate with the Spanish admiral. As English sailors without a license to trade in Spanish waters, Hawkins and his men might easily have been arrested. Instead, they arranged to exchange hostages. "But I don't trust these Spaniards," whispered Hawkins to Drake. "Keep your men ready for action!"

Hawkins was right. The Spaniards had prepared an ambush. Few of Drake's

shipmates escaped the bloody massacre that followed. As he sailed for home, Drake looked back in horror and fury at the shattered remains of the English ships which littered the harbor. He never forgave the Spanish for their treachery at San Juan.

English and Spanish rivalries

England and Spain fought during the 16th century because of their many differences. First, there was religious conflict: Spain was Catholic, while England had recently become Protestant. The Spanish kings saw it as a sacred duty to enforce the Catholic faith throughout Europe, by conquest if necessary. Second, England envied Spain's vast, wealthy colonies in the New World. The English wanted a share of that wealth, and the right to trade freely with the Spanish settlers, too. Third, a strong sense of national pride was developing in each country. This was encouraged, especially by Queen Elizabeth, because it took people's minds off troubles at home. Finally, there was the clash of personalities, policies and beliefs between two proud, stubborn monarchs, Elizabeth and Philip.

Far horizons

It was four years after the disastrous ambush at San Juan de Ulua. Drake and his men were back in the hot, unhealthy lands of Central America. They fought their way through thickets of lush green undergrowth, hacking a path with knives and machetes. Friendly Cimaroon Indian guides helped them find their way. At last, they came to a clearing.

"Right, men, we'll rest here a while," said Drake. "Now, John, let's have a look at that chart. We ought to be getting near the coast before long." His nephew came running with the precious map looted from the Spanish settlers. He knew better than to dawdle when Drake gave orders. For Drake was the leader of his expedition, and captain, too, of his own ocean-going ship. On the long Atlantic crossing, his men had soon learned to respect his skill as a sailor, but also to fear his anger if they disobeyed him.

While he studied the map, Drake recalled his earlier voyages to this unexplored New World in the west. Then, he had heard tales of the rich lands of Chile and Peru, with their fabulous mines where gold and silver were quarried from deep in the earth. He had seen new lands, new plants, new peoples and new creatures, all more wonderful than anything in his wildest dreams.

He felt sure that this was where his future lay. By attacking the Spanish towns and treasure ships, he could, like Hawkins, make himself rich and famous. Even better, he could avenge his comrades massacred by the Spaniards at San Juan de Ulua, and strike a blow for the Protestant cause.

So here he was, in this steamy jungle clearing, looking for another chance to attack the Spanish, and for new riches to plunder. Drake knew that the ships from Peru would soon arrive in Panama, to meet the fleet from Spain that had sailed across the Atlantic Ocean. Before long, the Spanish mule trains would pass nearby, with their heavy loads of treasure bound for Spain. But it was weary waiting and easy to miss their prey in this clammy, sickly jungle.

Drake stretched and clambered to his feet. It was time they moved on. Slowly they trudged along a winding path, toward the crest of a low ridge of hills. The Cimaroons had told him that there was an excellent view from there. "You can see two oceans!" they said.

Drake reached the hilltop, and climbed up into the spreading branches of a huge tree. He peered eastward and could just see the dull gleam of the gray Atlantic on the horizon. Then he turned to look westward. His eyes caught the sparkle of sunlight on the blue water, and he gazed in awe. There it was, the great Pacific Ocean, about which such fantastic travelers' tales were told. The sight took his breath away, and his heart beat faster. No English ships had yet sailed in these waters, for the King of Spain claimed them for his own. "One day," vowed Drake, fervently, "I'll sail my English ship on that Spanish sea. Let God be my witness!"

13

A secret meeting with the queen

It was a bright, breezy Sunday morning in April. The townsfolk of Plymouth hurried to church, as all Queen Elizabeth's loyal subjects were duty bound to do. A few stayed away; some through laziness, some because of illness, others because they secretly kept to the old Catholic faith they had been brought up with.

One man simply could not bear to be indoors on such a brilliant spring morning. He took his dog for a walk on Plymouth Hoe, a hill overlooking the harbor. Idly, he watched the ships move back and forth. A rather bedraggled frigate of Spanish design

seemed to be coming in. He looked again, more closely. A Spanish ship was most unusual. He scanned the rigging to see what flags she flew. He looked yet again. Surely that was Drake's flag? It was well-known in Plymouth. But it was over a year since Drake had sailed away, and no one knew where he was. Could he really be coming home? Yes! there was the familiar stocky figure waving from the stern deck. The watcher on the shore raced toward the town and rushed into the church, to the astonishment of his fellow-citizens. "Drake's back!" he panted. "Drake's come home!"

The preacher was in the middle of his sermon. He looked none too pleased at being interrupted, but few church goers heard his complaints. They had all rushed down to the harbor to gaze at the captured Spanish ship and greet their local hero.

However welcome he might be in Devon, to Queen Elizabeth and her advisers Drake presented a tricky problem. Like everyone else in England, they were full of admiration for his skill and daring, and secretly they were delighted when he did anything – like capturing one of their ships – to irritate the Spaniards. But officially, England and Spain were not at war, and so Elizabeth could not openly support Drake. Once news of Drake's return spread through the land, the Spaniards in London hurried to court to demand that the queen punish him. "He's nothing better than a pirate!" they exclaimed, angrily.

Fortunately, the Spaniards never got to hear that Drake and Queen Elizabeth had met in secret to discuss his next venture. The queen promised Drake her protection. But she also warned him that she could not come to his rescue if anything went seriously wrong. She would not start a war with Spain on his behalf.

Drake was satisfied. For once, his mind was on more than war; he was planning an expedition. Whatever the Spaniards might say, he was setting out for the Pacific Ocean!

The last place on earth

The sailors had never seen such a terrifying storm. Hurricane-force winds screamed in the rigging. Squalls of rain battered the decks. All around, the mountainous seas reared up in white-topped crests higher than the masts. The *Golden Hind,* Drake's flagship, pitched and bobbed helplessly like a cork. At one minute she lurched dizzily on the top of a wave, at another she slithered sickeningly down into a trough. All around, the gigantic swell threatened to engulf her. She had lost touch with her sister ships. Probably they were wrecked by now. Who could tell how much longer the *Golden Hind* herself could withstand such a pounding by wind and water?

Her crew huddled below decks. "They call this ocean the last place on earth, and I'm not surprised," said one old sailor, dismally. "I must have been mad to sign up for a second voyage with Drake," said another. "He's a great sailor, true enough, and good to us crewmen, but to take us so far from home . . . it's not right! Nothing was said about going into the Pacific until we were well out to sea." He spat in disgust. "I wouldn't have come if I'd known what I was letting myself in for! If it's adventure and plunder that the master wants, then surely there's enough of that in the West Indies. We don't need to go to Chile and Peru as well!"

A muffled groan came from a dark corner, where one of their mates was being horribly sick. "Let me lay my bones peacefully in a Plymouth churchyard," he moaned, "not at the bottom of some heathen ocean, thousands of miles from England." He rolled over, and turned his face to the wall. Drake's nephew John spoke up. "Where's your spirit, man?" he said. "This storm can't last much longer, and we're in a good strong ship. We'll survive!"

Above them, the deck planking creaked and groaned ominously. Even John glanced nervously toward the sides of the vessel, where water was beginning to seep through into the hold. "Some hope of surviving this storm!" replied the sick man. "We'll not last long in these God-forsaken seas! You'd better say your prayers, my lad, before it's too late!"

The hatch cover flew open suddenly, letting in a deluge of rain and salt spray. Drake himself staggered in, soaked to the skin. He looked exhausted, but full of confidence and courage. "The wind is dropping, heaven be praised!" he exclaimed. "We've sighted land to the north. Cheer up, my brave lads! We'll live to sail in the Pacific Ocean, after all!"

A gentleman pirate

The *Cacafuego's* captain shaded his eyes against the sun. Was that a sail on the horizon? He'd heard rumors that Drake was in the Pacific. He hoped it wasn't true. That man was a devil! The *Cacafuego* glided on across the Pacific. She was sailing home from Peru to Panama, heavily laden with rich treasures to be shipped to Spain. The captain looked again at the distant ship. It was no closer, even though its sails were fully spread to catch the wind. It was probably a harmless coastal trader, but he'd keep an eye on it, all the same.

Drake peered anxiously over the *Golden Hind's* stern. Below, in the water, floated a strange mixture of objects tied to the ship with tow ropes: buckets, old mats, and wooden boxes. The bosun smiled. "Excellent!" he said. "All that junk in the water has slowed us right down. That old pirate trick never fails. Those Spaniards'll think we're too slow to catch them." Drake laughed. "We'll soon prove them wrong! The *Cacafeugo* is the richest prize we've found, and she'll not escape us!"

They trailed the *Cacafuego* at a safe distance all day. That evening, after dusk, Drake cut the tow ropes and the *Golden*

Hind sprang forward, racing towards her prey.

In the dark, the Spaniards could not see that she was English. So, thinking the *Golden Hind* was friendly, the *Cacafuego's* captain hurried to greet her, glad of an escort for the last leg home. His words rang across the still water "Ahoy! Who are you? What is your home port?"

Drake's reply made his blood run cold. "We are English! Lower your sails and heave-to, or we'll send you to the bottom of the ocean!"

The Spanish captain would not give up so easily. "Come aboard and do the job yourself!" he yelled defiantly. But he knew it was hopeless. His ship was too slow and heavy to escape Drake's attack. Soon, the Spanish captain was being led captive into Drake's cabin, while Drake's men took over his ship. The English sailors gasped at the sight of the treasure they found. As well as exotic fruits and sugar, they discovered precious stones, jewelry, gold coins and bars, and over 26 tons of silver.

On board the *Golden Hind,* the Spanish captain was received with great courtesy. He was given a seat of honor at Drake's table, where delicious food was served on silver plates, while Drake's musicians played soothing music. Drake might be little better than a pirate, thought the Spanish captain, but he treated his prisoners like gentlemen!

The Spice Islands

Drake's men put the Spanish captain ashore after a few days, and continued their voyage, destroying and looting where they could. They sailed past Panama, where Drake had first caught sight of the Pacific, on to the mysterious lands of the north. The men complained bitterly about the cold and damp. After weeks sailing in tropical heat, the chilly winds and sea fogs were hard to bear. At last, they set up camp on shore, and traded with some of the Indians they met there. Drake put up a sign claiming the land, which he named New Albion, for England and for Queen Elizabeth.

But soon it was time to leave. Their ships were repaired and refilled with water and fresh provisions. No English ship had ever sailed where Drake planned to lead his men. They said farewell to the Indians, and set off for the unknown.

The *Golden Hind* sailed on and on westward, across the wide, empty Pacific. It was two months since they had left the coast of North America, and their supplies were running low. Many of the crew were sick, with fevers and through lack of fresh food and water. Some had died.

"Land! Land ahead!" cried the lookout. Excitedly, they lowered a small boat to row across to the islands. But they were met by a ferocious volley of sticks and stones. The rowers were lucky to escape alive. Dismally, they sailed on. Soon some more islands appeared on the skyline. Drake consulted his charts. "These should be the Spice Islands," he said. "Now we'll see whether those Portuguese traders' stories are true! Anyway, we should be safer here!"

No travelers' tales could have prepared them for the royal welcome they received. The sultan himself was rowed out to greet them, surrounded by his courtiers, all elegantly dressed. The sultan stood up in his royal canoe and bowed graciously. Drake returned the greeting and, after they had exchanged gifts, Drake ordered his musicians to strike up a rousing tune, as if they were playing for a royal occasion at home. Their music pleased the sultan so much that he asked for the band to be lowered down to sea in a small boat to entertain him while he and his courtiers sailed in a stately procession around the bay.

Drake and his men stayed several days in the islands, while they took on fresh provisions and Drake arranged some profitable business deals with the local spice merchants. Then, all too soon, it was time to set sail again. They were still a long way from home!

Arise, Sir Francis!

Drake arrived back in Plymouth nearly three years after he had set sail. Of the five ships and 164 men he had sailed with, only one ship and its crew returned. But they returned in triumph. Drake was the first English captain to sail around the world. He had seen many strange and marvelous sights. He had plundered many Spanish ships and possessions. He had captured an enormous fortune in treasure. He had survived storms, shipwrecks, and won his crew's respect and loyalty. Drake was a hero.

Even so, he was unsure how Queen Elizabeth and her courtiers would greet him. How had the news of his attacks on Spanish civilians and Spanish property been received at court? Would the queen disown him and have him thrown into prison for piracy? Or would she praise him as a gallant soldier?

Drake was uneasy until he was invited to meet the queen. Elizabeth was very anxious, the royal messenger said, to congratulate Drake on his adventurous voyage and to see some of the treasures he had brought home with him. Drake took the hint and hurried to London with a magnificent gift of Spanish gold bars and coins for the queen. He gave her other presents too: a crown studded with massive emeralds from Peru and a fabulous diamond cross.

The queen listened eagerly to Drake's stories about his travels. When he told about his attacks on the Spanish, she was delighted. "My pirate!" she said. "You have done me great service. Bring your ship to London,

and I will come on board to visit you."

The travel-stained *Golden Hind* was brought around the coast from Plymouth to London, and thoroughly cleaned for the royal visit. At last the great day dawned. The queen's bodyguard mingled with the excited spectators, who flocked to the quayside to cheer their hero.

Queen Elizabeth arrived, followed by a grand procession of courtiers. The queen inspected the ship, and then, in front of the vast crowd, commanded Drake to kneel. She gave her jeweled sword to her escort for the day, the French Duc d'Alençon, and told him to tap Drake lightly on the shoulders with it, according to the old custom of bestowing knighthood. But first she joked with Drake. "Shall I cut off your head, because you are a lawless pirate?" she said. "No, I shall make you a knight! England needs men like you! You are worthy of this great honor! Arise, Sir Francis Drake!"

Ruler of half the world

"Another messenger has arrived from the Low Countries, sire." The royal secretary hovered nervously in the doorway of King Philip's study. The king stifled a yawn. It was very late. "Show him in," he said, wearily. "We must see what news he brings."

King Philip II of Spain was the most powerful man in Europe and ruler of half the known world. From his father, he had inherited vast lands in Germany, Austria and the Low Countries. From his grandparents, he had inherited Spain and almost half of Italy. By conquest, and by order of the Pope, he was emperor of the new found lands in North and South America.

Many lesser men would have been content simply to enjoy the great wealth brought in by all these lands, but not Philip.

By nature, he was a shy, scholarly man, who hated pomp and ceremony, and preferred to live quietly, away from the noise and bustle of his court. But he felt called by destiny to fulfill a sacred duty rather than please himself. He viewed his empire as a God-given trust, to be defended and watched over.

As he wrote to his daughters, whom he loved dearly, and whose company he missed when he was closeted in his gloomy study, "I have a duty to defend the Holy Catholic Faith against those wicked people who would attack it. In so many parts of my empire I find Protestant heretics, who seek to put their own mistaken views in place of the Church's teachings. Why, only the other day, here in Spain itself, I felt obliged to

attend an Auto da Fé, where we burned a stubborn heretic. I must show the people how much I care for their souls. And now, what is worse, those Protestants in the Low Countries want to break away from the empire and govern themselves. My children, it is a heavy burden to be a king!"

Night after night saw King Philip sitting up late in his study, perpetually troubled and watchful over the state of his far-flung lands. "He fusses like a mother hen," confided one of his courtiers. "What other king would fret so over all the details? He trusts nobody and leaves nothing to chance." And so, even though Philip worked day and night to do his duty, the empire was badly run. It took weeks for Philip, working almost single-handedly, to digest all the information he received from his local officials and months for him to come to a decision. The delays grew so bad that a saying became common in many corners of the empire: "If death came from Spain, we should all live forever!"

The news that the messenger brought that night was most worrying. Drake's attacks on Spanish colonies in the New World were expensive and irritating, but now it seemed that the English and the Dutch were working together to drive the Spaniards out of northern Europe. King Philip had sent one of the most famous battle-commanders in Europe, the Duke of Parma, to lead the Spanish forces in the Low Countries. Parma took thousands of brutal mercenary soldiers with him; men from many different lands who joined his army for the pay and plunder it offered, or simply because they liked fighting. But even these troops were finding it hard to win the fight against the Dutch rebels and their English allies.

"There's no help for it, sire," said Philip's secretary. "Who knows what devilment Elizabeth and Drake are cooking up between them? We have no choice. We must prepare for war with England!"

Revenge at last!

The galleon *Elizabeth Bonaventure* heaved and swayed at anchor. Below deck, in his cabin, Drake hurried to finish the letter he was writing. "The wind commands me away," he scribbled. "Our ships are under sail." He added a few more lines and put down his quill pen. His loud voice rang around the ship as he called for a messenger. That April night in 1587, Drake and his fleet of 30 ships sailed out of Plymouth, and set course for Spain.

In London, the queen and her advisers discussed the next move. "We can't risk provoking Spain into an all-out attack on us," they said, "our ships aren't ready to fight. We mustn't let that hothead Drake take matters into his own hands again. Who knows what trouble he'll cause!" They sent their fastest messenger to find Drake and give him orders not to attack the Spaniards. The messenger rode day and night until, muddy and exhausted, he reached Plymouth. "Where's Drake?" he panted. "I've an urgent message for him, from the queen!" But he was too late. Drake had already left.

Eighteen days later, Drake's fleet anchored off the Spanish coast. They could just see the enemy harbor of Cadiz on the far horizon. There would be rich plunder there, to seize from the vessels peacefully at anchor behind the strong harbor walls.

Drake thought gleefully of ships to attack and of prisoners to be captured and ransomed. He summoned his captains to a council of war. "Now's our chance to destroy the Spanish warships – and their navy's stores – while they're still getting ready to attack us!" he said. "The last thing they expect just now is an English raid! King Philip will be the laughing stock of Europe when we sink his ships in his own harbor." Drake smiled as he imagined the proud king's disgrace. He wondered what Queen Elizabeth and her stuffy courtiers would think.

The other captains felt that a sudden raid would be too risky. "If you ask me," said Captain Borough, "we'd do better to wait until tomorrow. By then, we can work out a proper battle plan." But Drake ignored him. "Back to your ships!" he commanded. "We'll take those Spanish dogs by surprise tonight!"

The English fleet advanced into Cadiz Bay. At first, the townspeople had no idea of what was about to happen. Then a rumor spread through town. "El Draque . . . El Draque! The English Dragon has come to attack us!" They ran, terrified, to take shelter in the old castle. At sea, the Spanish sailors bravely tried to defend their harbor, but their old-fashioned galleys were no match for the brutal English cannon. The rowers simply could not get close enough to attack the English ships with their galleys' great bronze battering rams. Soon, the water was full of shattered oars and fragments of timber. Groaning, mutilated sailors struggled briefly before sinking beneath the waves.

Drake sailed on into the inner harbor. There he found a great galleon, the pride of the Spanish fleet. Soon Drake's men had set her ablaze. By nightfall, the water was red with fire and blood, the harbor strewn with wrecked ships.

"This is El Draque's work," said the Spaniards, in horror. "He is evil. All that he cannot plunder, he destroys!"

The treasure ship

Drake's fleet sailed triumphantly out of Cadiz harbor. "Our next target," he told his crew, "is Sagres Castle. From there, we will be able to command the whole coastline. And after that," he added, with a wicked grin, "we make for Lisbon. We must destroy the fleet that the Spaniards are building there." He thumped his fist down hard on the table, making those standing nearest to him jump. "We must fight to defend our country and our Protestant faith! We will not be safe until the Spanish empire is destroyed!"

They quickly captured the castle. Afterwards, Drake stayed ashore with some of his men, while the smaller ships in his fleet chased the Spanish coastal vessels which were busy ferrying timber to the great naval dockyard at Lisbon. "If they can't get wood, then they can't build ships or barrels to store food and water in," explained Drake. "We'll burn their wood and stop them sailing to attack us!"

Drake's fleet set off for Lisbon with high hopes. But they were disappointed. The great harbor was well-defended and could be reached only through a narrow channel whose twists and turns were a closely guarded secret. Drake had no wish to run aground within range of banks of Spanish cannon, so he ordered his ships to set sail once more for the open sea.

But it was not long before he heard news which drove all thoughts of failure from his mind. A huge cargo ship, belonging to the King of Spain himself, and named the *San Felipe* in his honor, was due home from the Far East. She would be laden with unimaginable riches. Most of Drake's other captains wanted to return home, since the weather was growing stormy, but Drake was adamant. They would ambush her!

Later, people said that Drake must have had magical powers to know where to lie in wait for his prize, but Drake said he had simply studied the weather and the tides. At any rate, he managed to capture the *San Felipe* on the open sea, and seize great quantities of treasure. The great weight of the *San Felipe's* cargo made her slow and cumbersome, and her guns were fixed too high along her sides to damage the smaller English ships. They darted beneath her gunfire to shoot with their smaller, more accurate cannon. After a brief battle, in which several of her crew were killed, the *San Felipe* surrendered. As Drake said, it was another "happy success against the Spaniards."

Getting ready for war

The docks in Lisbon were a scene of feverish activity. The hectic sound of hammering rang in the air, mingling with the shouted orders of the overseers and the murmured prayers of the priests. At long last, King Philip had decided to launch an attack on England!

Here at the docks, a great fleet was being made ready for war. Every available ship was gathered in Lisbon, waiting to sail north toward England. They would carry battalions of well-armed soldiers, all eager to invade the heretic island. Some ships would rendezvous with the Spanish troops already in the Low Countries, and ferry them across the Channel to the poorly defended Kent and Essex marshes. Then they would march on London and remove the wicked heretic Queen Elizabeth from her throne. Some of the Spanish commanders imagined the scenes of rejoicing that would take place when the captured queen was led in disgrace through the streets of Madrid.

Next, of course, they would capture that evil pirate, Drake. No death would be too painful for him! Yes, Spain would have her revenge for all those years of humiliation!

They would pay Drake back for all those attacks on Spanish lives and property! And, as the Spanish priests explained in their sermons, this Armada would be the first blow in a holy war, a crusade to reclaim England for the Catholic church. The ships' banners were solemnly blessed at a special service by the Bishop of Lisbon, and all the sailors confessed their sins before they went on board ship. They were to be righteous warriors in a great cause! A Spanish victory would remove, once and for all, any English threat to Spain's far-flung empire. What's more, it would increase the power and glory of Philip, Spain's "Most Catholic King."

This, then, was what King Philip and his advisers planned, closeted together in his study in the remote royal palace in the center of Spain. It was just what Drake had foreseen and what he hoped to prevent by his attacks on Lisbon and Cadiz. His raids had left the Spanish fleet disastrously short of good timber for making barrels for food and drinking water, and his capture of the *San Felipe* had left the Spanish treasury dangerously empty. But this did not stop King Philip from pressing ahead with his invasion plans. Like Drake, he saw the war between their two nations as his sacred duty, which could not be shirked. They had to fight.

The Spanish are coming!

"I have not in my life known better men possessed with gallanter minds." Drake was writing from Plymouth, where he was in charge of the Western Squadron of the fleet that was being assembled to defend England against the Spanish attack. The whole country was seized with anti-Spanish fever, and, like Drake's crew, was eager to see some action against the invaders.

Drake himself pleaded with the queen to be allowed to lead another attack on Lisbon. "Our best hope is to destroy the Spanish fleet before it sails," he argued. "We must seek our peace by a resolute and determined war. Once the Spaniards set sail, it will be difficult to stop them from landing in England. Our soldiers are keen, but remember, they don't have much experience in fighting off invaders!" Eventually, the queen allowed him to set off toward Spain, but his fleet was driven back by heavy gales. Drake was bitterly disappointed, but this defeat by the weather made him even more determined to succeed in the end. With the other naval commanders, he discussed battle plans, checked his ships' supplies of food and ammunition, and waited impatiently until it was time for action.

On land, the army commanders were also busy preparing to meet the Spanish attack. Local officers mustered their troops and had them begin practice target shooting and hand-to-hand fighting. Anyone suspected of being a Catholic was kept under close watch by the government's secret agents. All along the south coast of England, a chain of beacons was built, to be lighted as a signal when the hated Armada sailed into view. These beacons were watched over night and day by specially appointed guards. Little flyboats scurried out from south coast ports, looking out for the first sight of the invading fleet.

At last, in mid-July 1588, the long-awaited news came. The Armada had left Spanish waters and was heading northwards! The fleet had been sighted off the Scilly Isles! Beacon after beacon leaped into flame in the summer twilight. The Spaniards were coming!

The Armada was made up of 132 vessels, of all shapes and sizes. There were great fighting galleons and galliasses; heavy transport hulks; wallowing, cumbersome East Indian merchant ships; and a whole flotilla of tiny craft. It was led by one of the greatest nobles in all Spain, the Duke of Medina Sidonia. He was highly-respected, intelligent and honest, but he was no sailor. He had protested to King

Philip that he was not the right man for the job – apart from his lack of experience, he suffered badly from seasickness – but, typically, Philip had refused to listen to reason.

Slowly, majestically, the Armada advanced closer toward England. But Drake was not afraid. He kept his fleet in harbor until the Armada had passed Plymouth. He knew that the Spaniards were sailing into unfamiliar waters, and that he could more easily attack them from the rear. He would have the advantage of the wind that way, as well. Local people could hardly believe how calm Drake was. "Do you know," they marveled, "that when the news of the approaching Armada was brought to him, people said that Drake was playing a game of bowls?" "Let them pass!" he said. "There's plenty of time, I'll finish this game first, and then we'll defeat them!"

The warrior queen

Queen Elizabeth, splendidly clothed in velvet embroidered with gold and jewels, rode on a noble white horse around the parade ground at Tilbury. Her soldiers cheered and waved their hats. Here was their great queen, the symbol of England itself, come to visit them before they went into battle.

Over the past ten days, a whole new army camp had been built at Tilbury, to house the soldiers waiting to defend England against the Armada. Now the Spanish invasion fleet was advancing toward them. Who knew what would happen next?

At sea, Drake and the other naval commanders were chasing the Spaniards up the Channel, seeking out the weakest ships to capture or destroy. News reached the soldiers of battles off Portland Bill and the Isle of Wight, but the hoped-for victory had not yet happened. Rumors flew throughout Europe: the Spanish were defeated, the

Spanish had won! Drake was victorious, Drake was captured, Drake was dead!

Elizabeth could see that these rumors were frightening her soldiers at Tilbury. What could she do to restore their courage? She would make a speech to inspire them, one which they would never forget!

"I know I have the body of a weak and feeble woman," she said, "but I have the heart and stomach of a king, and of a king of England too, and I think foul scorn that Parma or Spain or any prince of Europe should dare to invade the borders of my realm!"

It was a magnificent performance, but the battle for England was not being fought at Tilbury. Rather, the fate of all England, from Queen Elizabeth herself down to the humblest of her subjects, depended on what happened at sea. Would Drake and the other commanders be able to defeat the great Armada, after all?

Countdown to disaster: the Armada timetable

January 1586	Philip decides to invade England
April 1587	Drake's raid on Cadiz
May 30, 1588	Armada leaves Lisbon
July 29	Armada sighted off Isles of Scilly
July 30	English fleet sails from Plymouth
July 31	Drake captures flagship *Nuestra Señora del Rosario*
August 2–5	Minor battles between English and Spanish fleets
August 6	Spanish and English fleets anchor off Calais
August 7–8	English attack with fireships
August 8	Battle off Gravelines; Spanish fleet scattered
August 12	English chase Spanish north into stormy seas; chase abandoned August 13
August 18	Elizabeth's speech at Tilbury
Mid-August – September	Armada limps home round Scotland and Ireland; many ships wrecked
September 23	Spanish commander reaches home

Devil ships!

Drake paced up and down on deck. Things were not going well. True, he had managed to capture a rich and important galleon, and there had been several skirmishes in which the English sailors had showed that they were better than the Spaniards at handling ships in these tricky northern waters. Their guns were quicker, too, to load and fire, and more accurate. Best of all, they could fire long-distance. But now, both sides were running short of powder and shot, and the English had still not managed to shake the Armada out of its tight, crescent-shaped defensive formation. "If they stay like that," thought Drake, "then we'll never stop them."

The Armada had reached the narrow seas between England and France, and lay at anchor outside Calais harbor. "It's only a matter of time," thought Drake, "before the Spanish admiral makes contact with their troops on shore. That will mean disaster for England! Those troops are ferocious, and Parma, their commander, is the best general in Europe. They've spent years fighting the Dutch, and hate all Protestants. Our English troops at Tilbury are certainly keen, but most of them have never seen any fighting. God knows how they'll behave in a real battle!"

As darkness fell, the English commanders held a council of war. They agreed with Drake. The time had come to strike hard against the Spaniards. They would attack with their most terrifying weapons – fireships! Eight boats were crammed with anything – tar, straw, old rope – that would burn. Their guns were loaded with double quantities of shot and their sails were hoisted ready to catch the wind.

Long past midnight, the Spanish lookouts saw a nightmare vision drifting slowly over the sea. Fireships! Devil ships driven by wind and tide toward the sleeping fleet! Ghostly, unmanned ships, which no power on earth could halt, spitting cannon balls and belching clouds of deadly fire and smoke. How could the Spanish escape? Behind them lay the shallow waters and cliffs of the French coast. To the south west lay the English warships, preparing to attack with their fearsome long-range guns. There was no time even to haul up the anchors. Panic-stricken, the Spanish captains cut their cables and scattered, racing away from the fireships and out toward the open sea.

On board the ships of the English fleet, Drake and his fellow commanders watched with grim satisfaction. At last, the Spanish defenses were breached. This was the chance they had all been waiting for! Now they could attack!

The miracle that came too late

"God has given us so good a day," wrote Drake, in rather shaky handwriting. He was exhausted, but triumphant. So much had happened that he feared he would fall asleep, pen in hand, before he was able to write all of it down.

Early that morning, through the mist, the English had seen the Spanish fleet in disorder, scattered by the deadly fireships. Right away Drake had launched a fierce attack on the Spanish flagship.

During the night, a great galliass, the *San Lorenzo,* had been driven ashore and was now totally wrecked, yielding rich prizes to

the English and boosting their hopes of victory. Seeing the danger of staying too close to the shore, the Spanish admiral tried to lead his ships out to safer, deeper waters. But Drake guessed his plans. He led his own fleet to where the Spaniards were gathering. Again and again the English ships swept round the battered remains of the great Armada, raking the ships with merciless cannon and musket fire. It was a brilliant, deadly display of seamanship. And, as so often in the past, luck was on Drake's side. The Spaniards were desperately short of gunpowder and shot. They could not fire back

to drive Drake's ships away. Soon, the other English commanders joined in the battle. They pounded the Armada ships with gunfire until the decks ran red with Spanish blood.

Next morning, the English were helped by a gusting north-west wind, too strong for any sailing ship to tack against. Slowly, relentlessly, the Spaniards were forced back toward the shallow waters off the Dutch coast. The terrified Spanish sailors could do nothing as their ships began to founder among the roaring breakers that thundered on the shore. They sank to their knees in prayer, convinced that they would soon perish beneath the cruel waves.

Then, to everyone's amazement, their prayers were answered. Suddenly, and miraculously, without warning, the wind shifted. The battered, blood-stained Spanish ships limped northward out to the open sea, chased by the English. The great Armada was saved from total destruction. Some of the Spanish ships would survive to fight later battles. But the Spaniards had lost their chance of victory. They had failed in their attempt to invade and conquer England. As they said, bitterly, "What use is a miracle when it comes too late?"

Defeat, death and dishonor

The Duke of Medina Sidonia came from an ancient, noble family. For himself, he might have chosen death with honor by a heroic rearguard action against the English. He might have turned to face Drake and the English gunners, rather than escape northward, blown by the following wind. But King Philip had given him the responsibility of commanding the whole Armada. Now that there was no chance of outright victory, it was better for him to lead his surviving men safely home than to risk any more lives in pointless fighting. His task was not yet over. The Armada was still a long way from home in perilous, unknown seas.

The English fleet chased the Spaniards northward for several days. They were finally forced to turn back by a violent storm off the Scottish coast. The English seamen had not defeated the mighty Armada in a single, glorious battle, as they had hoped. But they had succeeded in keeping England safe from the threatened Spanish invasion and in destroying a large part of the enemy's fleet. It was a great achievement, even if it did not seem so at the time. Later, when news of the Spanish failure spread through Europe, there was rejoicing at home and praise for the victorious commanders. There was even a special service of thanksgiving at St. Paul's Cathedral, in London.

Drake took part, along with all the other leaders of the English fleet, but his mind was already full of schemes to renew the fight against Spain. He was busy planning a new attack on Portugal. Drake continued his personal war against the Spaniards until the very moment of his death in 1596, worn out by fever on yet another raiding voyage to the West Indies.

All that lay in the future. In the summer of 1588, Medina Sidonia and the Armada ships were still struggling to make their way through the treacherous northern seas. Their vessels were damaged and leaking. The sailors were half-starved through lack of food and water and tormented by disease. They had no charts to guide them and no experience of sailing in the storm-tossed waters of the North Atlantic. Many Spanish ships perished in sudden squalls or were wrecked on the rocky western coasts of Scotland and Ireland. Thousands of sailors were drowned on the long voyage home, as their ships were dashed against cruel rocks and cliffs. Even when a few survivors did manage to struggle ashore, they were often brutally murdered.

The Spanish fleet that finally reached home in September 1588 was a mere shadow of its former glorious self. Out of the 132 ships that had set sail, only 68 reached port. And of the 30,000 sailors who had left home with such brave hopes, over a quarter were dead. Among the living, sickness and starvation had reduced them all to pale, feeble wraiths, not sparing even the great Medina Sidonia himself. When the Armada limped pitifully into the harbor at Corunna, he was almost too weak to stand, and hundreds of sailors died in the filthy, crowded quayside hostels, too ill and feeble to make the journey home to their waiting, grieving families. It was a tragic end to a bold, but misguided, adventure. The great Spanish Armada had ended in failure.

The course of the Armada

Weymouth

Portland Bill

Plymouth

Land's End

July 29
Armada first sighted by English ship

July 31
Plymouth

Rosario
captured by Drake

August 1
Portland Bill

ENGLISH CHANNEL

0   miles   100

Battles ✗

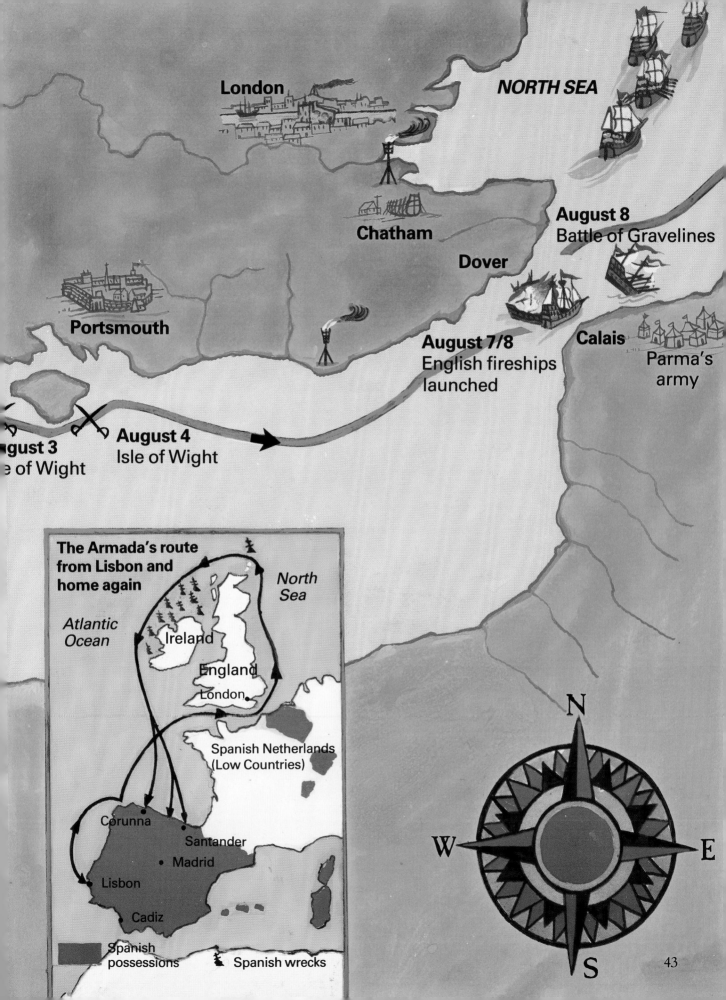

London

NORTH SEA

Chatham

Dover

August 8
Battle of Gravelines

August 7/8
English fireships launched

Calais

Parma's army

Portsmouth

ugust 3
e of Wight

August 4
Isle of Wight

The Armada's route from Lisbon and home again

Atlantic Ocean

North Sea

Ireland

England

London

Spanish Netherlands (Low Countries)

Corunna

Santander

Madrid

Lisbon

Cadiz

Spanish possessions

Spanish wrecks

N

W   E

S

43

Drake's voyage around the world

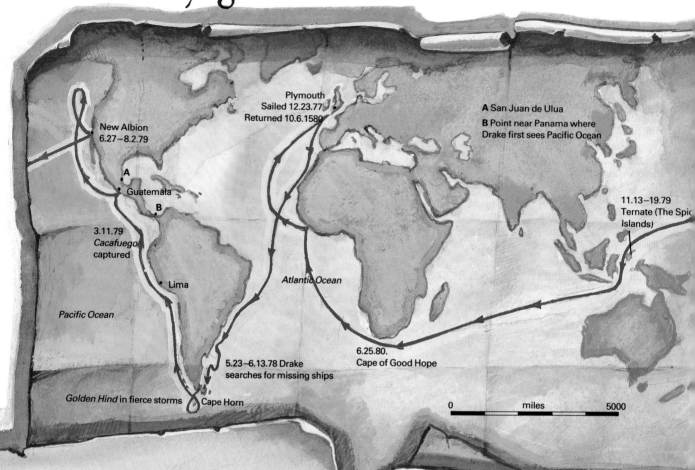

Plymouth
Sailed 12.23.77
Returned 10.6.1580

A San Juan de Ulua
B Point near Panama where
Drake first sees Pacific Ocean

New Albion
6.27–8.2.79

A

Guatemala

B

3.11.79
Cacafuego
captured

Lima

Pacific Ocean

Atlantic Ocean

11.13–19.79
Ternate (The Spice
Islands)

6.25.80.
Cape of Good Hope

5.23–6.13.78 Drake
searches for missing ships

Golden Hind in fierce storms   Cape Horn

0   miles   5000

Francis Drake: 1540/43–1596

1540/43 Francis Drake born in Devon; date of birth uncertain.

1549 Drake family flees Catholic uprising in Devon to settle on hulk at Chatham.

mid 1550s–late 1550s Drake apprenticed to the master of a small trading vessel. He inherits the vessel on his master's death.

1563 Drake moves to Plymouth to join his cousin, John Hawkins, in trading business.

1566 Drake's first voyage to West Indies with Hawkins.

1569 Drake and Hawkins attacked by Spanish at San Juan de Ulua.

1572 Drake's first voyage to West Indies as a commander; he vows to sail into the "Spanish" Pacific Ocean.

1575 Drake's first meeting with Queen Elizabeth. It is believed she encouraged him in his designs against Spain.

1577–80 Circumnavigation of the world: Drake leaves Plymouth in *Pelican* (later renamed *Golden Hind*) in command of five small ships. Only Drake's ship reaches the Pacific. Drake was the first man to sail his ship around the world. His fortune made, Elizabeth knights him on his return home.

1581 Drake becomes Mayor of Plymouth. He buys fine country mansion, Buckland Abbey, near Plymouth.

1585 Drake marries Elizabeth Sydenham, after death of first wife. Queen Elizabeth I places him in command of 25 ships, with orders to do as much damage as possible to Spanish ships and possessions.

1587 Drake raids Cadiz.

1588 Defeat of the Armada; Drake becomes a national hero.

1596 Drake's last years did not match the splendid success of his earlier life. His last voyage to the West Indies, yet again to attack the Spanish, was a failure; he died of fever and was buried at sea on January 28, 1596.

Glossary

Africa European traders sailed to the west coast of Africa in the 16th century to purchase gold, slaves and ivory.

Armada The Spanish word for "fleet of ships" or "national navy." Used to describe the fleet that set out to attack England in 1588.

Auto da Fé A public ceremony held in Spain where heretics were burned to death if they refused to change their beliefs.

Barrels Used to store essential supplies of food and water on board ship. They had to be made of properly seasoned (matured) wood. If not, the barrels would split open and the food would become rotten. Many of the supplies carried on the Armada ships spoiled because they were stored in barrels of unseasoned wood. Drake had destroyed all Spain's stocks of seasoned wood during his raids on Cadiz and Sagres the year before.

Beacons Used for sending signals, usually warnings, over long distances. They were built on high places, so they could be seen for miles around. In 1588, a great chain of beacons was built along the Channel coast and inland, to flash the news of the Armada's approach to the waiting troops and ships.

Cadiz An important port in Spain. Drake's daring attack on the Spanish shipping moored there boosted his reputation and made the Spaniards seem foolish and ill-prepared for war.

Calais A port in northern France. The Armada waited outside Calais harbor and planned to link up with the Spanish troops (who had been fighting the Dutch nearby) for a great invasion of England.

Catholics People who follow the teachings of the Roman Catholic Church.

Circumnavigation A word meaning "sailing around" – Drake was the first captain to sail his own ship around the world. The Portuguese explorer, Ferdinand Magellan, had been the first man to set off, in 1520, to sail around the world. He died on the voyage, but his crew completed the journey home.

Corunna The port in northern Spain to which Medina Sidona's ship returned in September 1588.

East Indies Countries in the Far East, between India and China.

Elizabeth Bonaventure The ship Drake sailed in when he attacked Cadiz. "Bonaventure" means "good fortune."

Fevers Sailors often fell ill on long voyages. Sometimes this was caused by the lack of wholesome food – especially fresh fruit and vegetables. Sometimes it was caused by unhygienic conditions on board ship. In the tropics, dangerous diseases were carried by mosquitos or caught from drinking polluted water.

Fireships Ships filled with quick-burning materials – tar, straw, etc. – and set on fire to drift toward the enemy; used by many navies in the 16th century. A new and more deadly type of fireship had been invented by an Italian engineer shortly before the Armada was planned. He used ships filled with gunpowder, which blew up as they approached the enemy, killing hundreds and wounding many more.

Flyboats Small, light sailing boats.

Galleon A sailing warship, built to be fast and easy to maneuver. English galleons were probably the best in Europe at the time of the Armada.

Galley A boat powered by men rowing, used mostly in calm Mediterranean waters. Galleys were often rowed by slaves or criminals, and were armed with a great bronze battering ram at the front. They carried large numbers of soldiers whose function was to board enemy ships and capture them.

Galliasses Sailing ships that could also be rowed. They could not sail as fast as galleons, but their oars enabled them to be rowed along when there was no wind, or when the wind was against them. Like galleys, they did not sail well in rough northern waters.

Gold and silver Large quantities of these precious metals were mined in the Spanish colonies in South America and shipped home to Spain. Drake captured many loads of Spanish gold and silver, and became a very rich man!

Golden Hind The name of the ship in which Drake sailed around the world. "Hind" means "deer." Drake named his ship after the crest (emblem) of one of the noblemen who had helped to finance the voyage. Previously it had been called the *Pelican*.

Guns Two types of guns were carried on Armada ships, cannons and muskets. Cannon, of various kinds, were mounted on wheels, with their muzzles sticking out of special holes (called gun ports) in the side of the ships. They fired heavy cannon balls. Muskets were fired by men holding them chest-high. They fired smaller shot. Both guns needed gunpowder, lighted by a spark, to fire their shot. English guns could fire more accurately over longer distances than many Spanish guns of the time of the Armada. More important, English gunners were more skillful, and the English commanders, especially Drake, used their ships' guns very cleverly to inflict maximum damage on their enemy.

Heretic A person said to hold incorrect religious beliefs.

Holy War A war fought to defend religious beliefs.

Hulk The hull of an old boat, no longer strong enough to go to sea. Often used to live in or for storage.

Lisbon The capital city of Portugal and a busy port. Spain conquered Portugal not long before the Armada was planned, and used Lisbon as a base for building the Armada.

Low Countries The lands now called the Netherlands. Often called Holland, although strictly speaking, that is the name of just one part of the Low Countries.

New Albion The name given by Drake to the temporary camp he built in California, and to the lands around it. He claimed these as a colony for England.

New World North and South America, including the lands now known as Canada, Alaska and the Caribbean. European travelers in the 16th century called it the New World because they had only just discovered it. To the people who already lived there, of course, it was not new at all!

Protestants People who follow the teachings of the Protestant Churches, which broke away from the Roman Catholic Church in the 16th century.

Sagres Castle An important fortress on the southern tip of Portugal (ruled by Spain at the time of the Armada). It was captured by Drake and used as a base from which to harass Spanish coastal shipping carrying materials to build the Armada.

San Juan de Ulua A Spanish island off the coast of Mexico, not far from the present-day town of Vera Cruz.

Spice Islands A group of islands in the East Indies, nowadays known as the Moluccas. Called the Spice Islands because of the many clove trees that grew there. European merchants visited them to buy these cloves, which they sold at high prices back home.

Sugar A rare and precious commodity in 16th century Europe. It was made from sugar cane, which only grows in hot countries, and had to be shipped to Europe from the East, like spices. Sugar and spices were great luxuries, but Drake was able to afford to serve them to his guests on board ship.

Tilbury A fortress and army camp in Essex, where the English troops were gathered to defend the south coast against the threat of invasion by the Spaniards.

West Indies The islands of the Caribbean. The first European explorers who landed in these islands thought they had traveled round the world and reached India. It was several years before they realized their mistake, and by then the name had stuck.

Index

Most of the places mentioned in the book are shown on the maps on pages 42–43 and 44.

Editor John Morton

Designer Jerry Watkiss

Production Rosemary Bishop

Factual Advisor Crispin Gill, historian of Plymouth

Printed and bound by Henri Proost, Turnhout, Belgium

Library of Congress Cataloging–in–Publication Data
Macdonald, Fiona.
     Drake and the Armada / written by Fiona Macdonald;
   illustrated by Chris Molan.
Includes index.
     p. — cm. — (Armada)
   Summary: A biography of the famous English sailor,
explorer, and battle commander who became a national
hero after helping to defeat the Spanish Armada in 1588.
     ISBN 0-531-19504-X
     1. Drake, Francis, Sir, 1540?–1596—Juvenile
literature. 2. Armada, 1588—Juvenile literature.   3. Great
Britain—History. Naval—Tudors, 1485-1603—Juvenile
literature.   4. Spain—History— Philip II, 1556–1598—
Juvenile literature.   5. Admirals—Great Britain—
Biography—Juvenile literature.   [1. Drake, Francis, Sir,
1540?–1596.   2. Admirals.   3. Explorers.   4. Armada.
1588.   5. Great Britain—History, Naval]—Tudors,
1485–1603.   6. Spain—History—Philip II, 1556-1598.] I.
Molan, Chris. II. Title. III. Series: Armada (New York,
N.Y.)
DA86.22.D7M23   1988
942.05′5′0924—dc19
[B]
[92]